What's the Biggest?

Weekly Reader

Children's Book Club

presents

What's the Biggest?
by *Barbara R. Fogel*

illustrated by Barbara Wolff

Random House / New York

To Janny, Jim, and Ed
who cheered me on

For helpful suggestions in the preparation of this book, the author
and the publisher are grateful to Dr. John Berrill, Department of
Zoology, University of Hawaii, and to Professor John A. Shimer,
Professor of Geology, Brooklyn College.

Contents

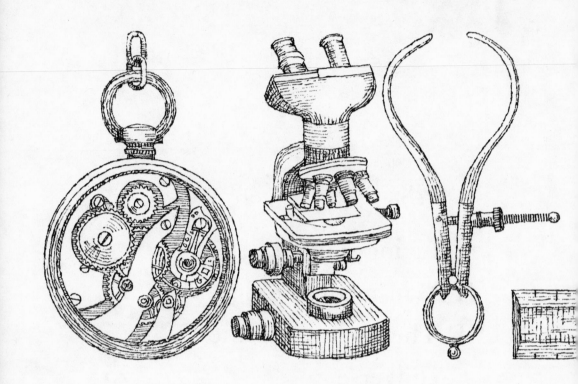

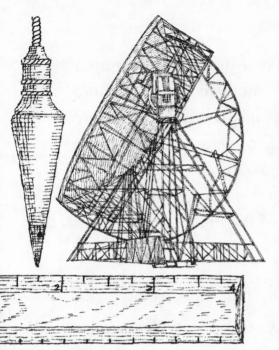
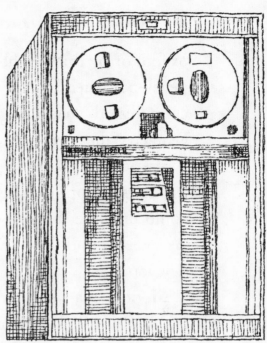

🎔 Big, Bigger, Biggest

When a primitive man first held a stone in each hand and tried to decide which stone was bigger, he started on the path to modern science. Science begins with questions. "How big?" was one of the first questions early man asked. A bigger cave, he knew, held a bigger family. A bigger pot held more water.

To find out how big, primitive men invented simple ways to measure—by the length of a hand or foot or by the weight of a stone. As civilization developed, men invented more accurate and more complicated measuring instruments. By using geometry they were able to measure the distance across water to learn the size of seas. Later, using the laws of optics, they built telescopes which could measure the size of the moon and the sun. As men found new ways to measure, science developed.

Modern man still asks how big—about more and more things. Today, to find out how tall a man or a house is, we still use a ruler much like the ones the early Egyptians used. But to find out how big viruses are, scientists now use electron microscopes which magnify two million times. Complicated telescopes can measure the size of a star millions of light-years away. To find the shape and size of the earth, scientists not only count yards or miles, but also observe the stars, and measure changes in gravity from place to place.

To measure we need accurate instruments. But we must also ask the right questions about size. In this book we will ask: What's the biggest? But first we must decide: biggest in what way? Do we mean heaviest? Do we mean tallest? Or do we mean able to do the biggest job? If we say one building is twice as big as another, do we mean it is twice as tall? Or that it covers twice as much area? Or that it holds twice as many people? Is the biggest computer the bulkiest or the most powerful?

How heavy a thing is depends partly on *where* it is. You would weigh less on the moon than you do on Earth. You would even weigh a little more at the North Pole than you would at the Equator. A pilot of a plane flying 4,000 miles an hour weighs four or five times his normal weight when the plane accelerates.

When we know what we want to measure and when we have the right instruments to measure it, we have taken the first two steps in science. Our rulers, microscopes, telescopes, and other measuring tools tell us facts—the blocks that science builds with. A scientist fits facts about size with other facts into theories which lead to more knowledge about the laws of nature.

Scientists are like detectives. When they know size, they have a clue to other questions and answers. Measuring the size of a tree tells something about its age. A seismograph which measures earthquakes reveals secrets of what is beneath the earth's crust. Finding their size helps scientists to understand the nature of the earth, the sun, and the stars. And measuring the distances between stars may even tell us how the universe began.

When we ask what's biggest, we not only measure; we also compare. Comparing one thing with another is one way scientists use facts. And when they have the facts and have compared them, they ask, "Why?"

In this book we will compare things to find out what's biggest and in what way. We will ask why some kinds of animals or bridges or buildings or stars are bigger than others. (Why can't an elephant be as big as a whale? Why can't a planet be as big as a star?) We will ask why things get as big as they do. (Why can a new bridge in New York be bigger than any earlier bridge?) We will ask why some things can't be bigger than they are. (Why is an ostrich too heavy to fly when a 200-ton airplane is light enough?) We will travel on many of the roads of science when we ask: What's the biggest?

·I·
Living Things

• What's the Biggest Land Animal?

Of all land animals living today, the elephant is the heaviest and most powerful. A big African bull elephant weighs 12,000 to 14,000 pounds—as much as 90 men. It is often twelve feet high at its shoulder, nearly as tall as a big moving van.

The elephant has skin an inch thick, about ten times as thick as our skin. Its trunk is strong enough to lift and toss away a small automobile, yet delicate enough to pick up a peanut or a blade of grass. It can drag several tons along the ground.

To nourish its huge body, the elephant must spend most of its time eating. It needs about 500 pounds of grass and leaves every day. And every day it must drink about 50 gallons of water, enough to fill 200 milk bottles.

One other animal is taller than the elephant—the giraffe. From his horn to his hoof, he may be over 19 feet high, taller than three men standing on each other's heads. A man could stand up straight between a giraffe's front legs.

Long ago there were land animals much taller than giraffes and much heavier than elephants. The biggest animals that ever lived on land were dinosaurs. The biggest dinosaur, the Brachiosaurus, was 80 feet long and weighed 50 tons— seven or eight times as much as an elephant. If it were alive today, it could look into a fourth-story window of a building.

These huge animals died off about 60 to 80 million years ago. Scientists are not sure why. One reason may be that the climate changed. As the weather gets hotter or colder, some plants cannot grow any more, and others take their place. Perhaps the plant-eating dinosaurs no longer had the food they needed. Meat-eating dinosaurs would then lose part of their food too —for they ate the plant-eating dinosaurs.

Or perhaps these giants could not stand hotter summers and colder winters. All the dinosaurs were reptiles. The blood of reptiles does not have its own warming system as our blood has. Whether a reptile is hot or cold depends on the temperature of the air or water.

If the days became colder, perhaps the dinosaurs found it harder to move. As reptiles become colder they get more sluggish. These monsters had trouble moving their enormous weight even on four thick legs. Cold weather may have made it harder to hunt food or defend themselves.

At the same time mammals began to compete for food. The first mammals who lived in the age of dinosaurs were no bigger than rats and mice today. But mammals have some advantages over reptiles. They are warm-blooded. They have automatic temperature controls, and their bodies stay at about the same temperature in either cold or warm weather. Their furry coats also help keep them warm. Protected against the weather, the mammals could hunt while the chilly dinosaurs dozed. Maybe the mammals even ate the dinosaur eggs.

Mammals have other advantages too. Their babies are born alive, not inside an egg. A mammal mother feeds her baby, protects it, and teaches it. Dinosaur babies had to manage for themselves.

Mammals also have bigger brains on the whole than reptiles have. One huge dinosaur had a brain weighing only 2½ ounces, less than the weight of a chocolate bar. All the dinosaurs had tiny brains. To learn many different things, an animal needs a bigger brain than it needs for learning just a few things. The human brain weighs about 3 pounds, twenty times as much as the brains of the enormous dinosaurs. With a bigger and more complicated brain, an animal can change its ways of doing things as the world changes.

• What's the Biggest Animal of All?

The biggest animal that ever lived is still alive today. This is the blue whale, also known as the sulfur-bottom whale. The biggest blue whale today weighs almost three times as much as the biggest dinosaur that ever lived. If the blue whale could stand on its tail, it would be as tall as a ten- or eleven-story building. One of the biggest blue whales ever measured weighed as much as eighteen of the biggest elephants—130 tons (260,000 pounds).

The whale is a mammal, not a fish. Unlike a fish, the whale has warm blood, lungs rather than gills, and it feeds its baby with milk from the

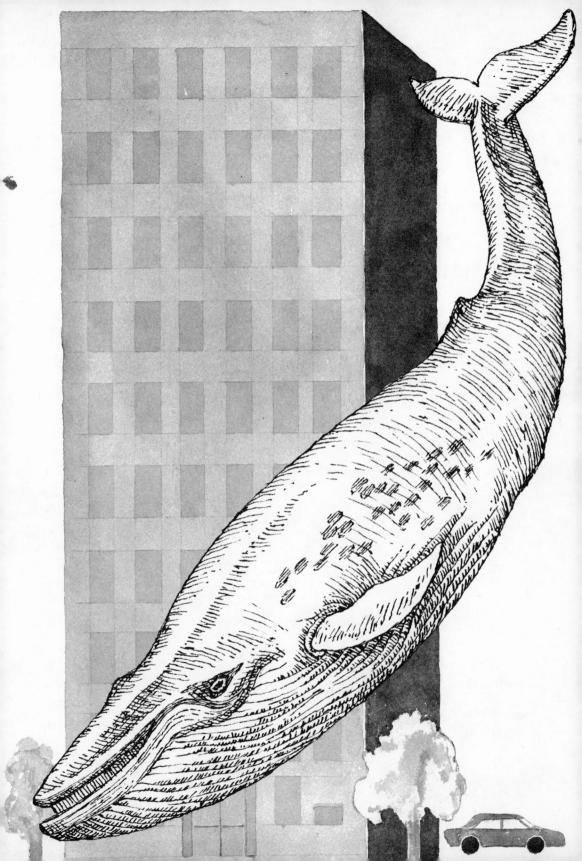

mother's body. The baby blue whale starts life from a tiny egg cell smaller than the period at the end of this sentence. It grows for a year inside its mother until it may weigh 16,000 pounds when it is born—as much as 2,000 human babies. From egg cell to birth, the blue whale has grown about 10 billion (10,000,000,000) times its original size in a year. Nothing else in the plant or animal kingdom grows that fast.

The baby blue whale is the biggest animal

The blue whale is much bigger than any dinosaur that ever lived. It would take about two thousand men to weigh as much as the largest blue whale.

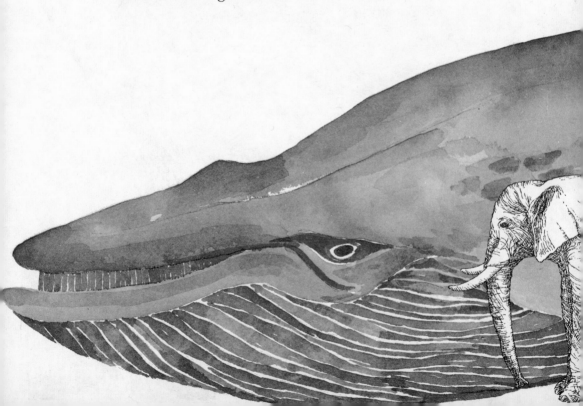

baby in the world. It is also the biggest baby compared to the size of its mother. Not all big animal mothers have big babies. A 500-pound black bear may have a baby that weighs only ½ pound and is very helpless. But a newborn blue whale may be 20 feet long and weigh more than the biggest adult elephant. It relies on its mother for food for 7 months, but it starts to do many things for itself right away.

Whales can grow as big as they do because the water supports their bodies. If they were on land, they would be too heavy to move. In fact, a whale stranded on a beach dies because his huge weight squashes his lungs so that he cannot breathe.

Whales, being mammals, cannot breathe under water as fish can. Some whales can plunge 3,000 feet down into the ocean. But before they dive, they fill their lungs with air. Blue whales can stay under water about half an hour before coming up for another breath.

A 100-ton blue whale has lungs weighing about one ton. But the whale does not stay under water so long only because its lungs are so big. In fact, the whale's lungs hold less air compared to its size than a man's lungs do compared to the man's size. Much bigger lungs would act like life preservers and keep the whale on top of the water.

Then how can a whale dive so long? One reason is that every time a whale breathes, it renews almost all the air in its lungs. We change only about one-fifth of the air in our lungs every time we breathe. Also, when a whale dives, his heart beats more slowly. This means he uses up oxygen more slowly while he is under water.

A blue whale must eat an enormous amount of food. Instead of teeth, its mouth contains two comb-like strainers which let through only tiny sea creatures. During the summer, the blue whale scoops up about a ton (2,000 pounds) a day of little shrimp-like animals and swallows them down its narrow throat.

The blue whale is the most powerful animal in the world. Usually it swims at about 14 miles an hour—as fast as a freighter—but it can race at 30 miles an hour. It has a pull of 400 horsepower. That's as much as 4,000 men all pulling together, or as much as a diesel locomotive.

With this power and speed, a blue whale can travel hundreds of miles in search of food.

Scientists put a mark on a blue whale one summer and found it a year later more than a thousand miles away.

• What's the Biggest Living Reptile?

Of course, not all reptiles died off with the dinosaurs. Some of their distant relatives—turtles, snakes, lizards, and crocodiles—are alive today.

In the days of the dinosaurs, when the weather got hot, little reptiles could crawl into holes between the rocks or dig holes in the ground to keep out of the sun. This may be one reason why smaller reptiles survived while the dinosaurs did not.

The heaviest reptile now living is the African crocodile. It lives in the Nile River and grows to be 16 feet—about as long as an automobile. Some of the biggest crocodiles may weigh more than 2,000 pounds.

How did these big reptiles go on living when the dinosaurs did not? The crocodile lives in the water, which helps support its heavy body. In addition, oceans, big rivers, and lakes don't get hot and cold as quickly as land does. Reptiles that spend their days floating in water do not feel climate changes as much as reptiles on land do.

Most of the heaviest and biggest reptiles today are found in rivers and oceans. Some sea turtles weigh 1,500 pounds. The only big reptile living on land, a 250-pound lizard called the Dragon of Komodo, lives in Indonesia where the weather stays fairly warm.

The biggest snake, the anaconda of South America, is as much at home in the water as on land. A big anaconda may weigh over 300 pounds, as much as a lion. The reticulate python from southeastern Asia weighs about 200 pounds. These two snakes, which may each be 30 feet in length, are the longest land animals living today.

They are also the only land animals that can gulp down whole animals as big as a man. They can eat at one time more food for their weight than any other land animal. In one meal they can eat 400 times what they need in a day. While big mammals such as whales and elephants must eat almost constantly, the giant snakes can go without eating for as long as a year after one big meal.

• What's the Biggest Fish?

The biggest fish found in fresh water is the Russian beluga sturgeon. It may grow to be 28 feet long and weigh as much as 3,000 pounds, more than the combined weight of twenty men. It makes its home in the Volga River.

The biggest of all fish is the whale shark—a true fish and no relation to the mammal whale. It

The whale shark can be as long as a freight car and weigh almost as much as the biggest dinosaur.

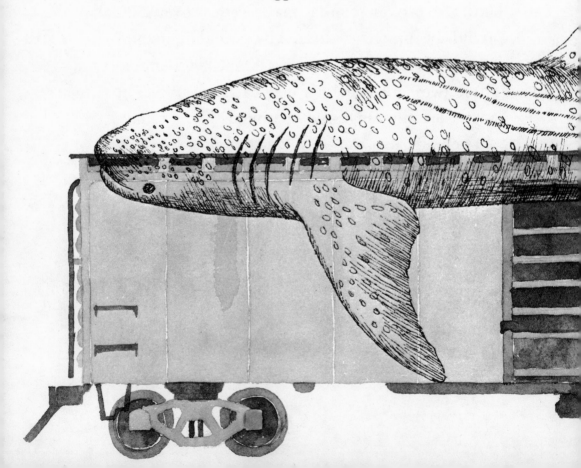

sometimes reaches fifty feet, as long as a railroad car, and can weigh 90,000 pounds, almost as much as the biggest dinosaur. Whale sharks live in southern waters and sometimes visit near Florida shores. But they eat only very small fish and seaweed and do not harm people.

Scientists have found fossils of very big shark teeth. These teeth make them think that some

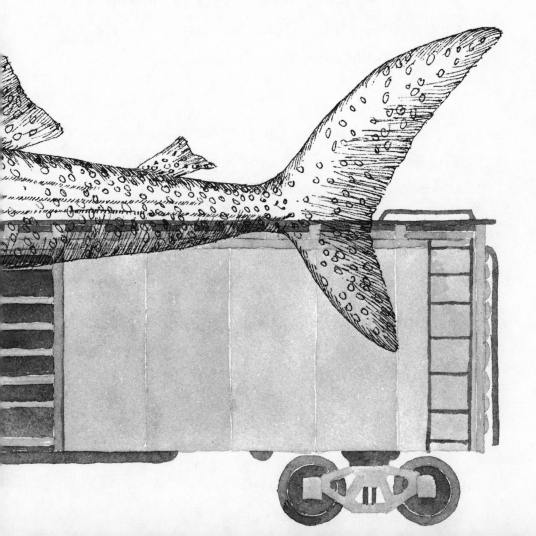

sharks, thousands of years ago, may have been twice as long as the whale shark and almost as long as the blue whale. But this is only a guess.

A mammal grows when it is young and then stops. A fish in a lake or sea, scientists think, probably continues to grow all its life, the way a tree does. We can find the same kind of fish, such as sturgeon, in many sizes. But we cannot always tell how old a fish is just by its size. Other things, such as where it lives and how much food it can find, determine how much the fish grows.

• What's the Biggest Bird?

The biggest bird of all is the ostrich. It can weigh 300 pounds or more. It grows eight feet tall.

The ostrich cannot fly. There are other big birds that cannot fly—emus, cassowaries, rheas, and kiwis. Scientists think the ancestors of these birds millions of years ago were smaller and flew like other birds. But most of the giant non-flying birds today live on islands where they have few enemies. Because no danger threatened them, they had no need to fly. Over millions of years these kinds of birds grew bigger and heavier, and their wings became weaker.

The ostrich, which lives on the African plains, does have hungry enemies such as lions and cheetahs. But the ostrich can run 50 miles an hour, faster than many of its enemies. Besides, the ostrich is so tall and has such good eyesight that it can see danger from far off. In fact, zebras and gnus often stay near an ostrich and use him as a lookout. When he runs, they run.

The ostrich lays the biggest egg in the world today. Its egg measures 6 to 9 inches long and weighs about three pounds. If it were empty, it could hold the insides of about 18 chicken eggs.

No egg can be very much bigger than an ostrich egg. The shell of a bird's egg must be strong enough to hold the egg and the developing baby bird. It must also be thin enough so that the chick growing inside the egg can breathe. An eggshell strong enough to hold together, say, a 15-pound egg would be too thick to let air in.

• ## What's the Biggest Flying Bird?

The heaviest flying bird is the trumpeter swan. This swan sometimes weighs as much as 40 pounds. Its wings can spread out ten feet. Next heaviest, the California condor, weighs up to 25 pounds and has a wingspread of about 9 feet.

The tallest flying bird is the whooping crane. These birds stand almost five feet tall, but they weigh less than the trumpeter swan or the California condor. Their wingspread is about 7 feet.

The albatross has the biggest wingspread of any bird. Its wings measure about 12 feet from the tip of one wing to the tip of the other—twice as far as the height of a man. The wing is a narrow strip only nine inches wide, ideal for soaring. By tacking with and then against the wind, the albatross can glide through the air for hours, hardly seeming to move its wings at all. Some have been known to follow a ship 3,000 miles. In a stiff wind the albatross can swoop over the sea at 100 miles an hour. But its long narrow wings have a disadvantage too: the albatross needs a long runway, such as the ocean surface, to take off. An albatross usually cannot take off from a ship's deck because the rail gets in its way.

From head to tail, the albatross is only about four feet long. It weighs about 20 pounds. Albatross parents care for and feed their babies until each one is very fat, heavier than the mother or father albatross. Then the parents fly off and leave their children. The baby albatross gets nothing more to eat. As it develops, it uses up its fat. At last, when the young albatross is much lighter and very hungry, it makes its first flight alone.

No flying bird weighs more than about 40 pounds—about one-eighth the weight of an ostrich. A bird *twice* as heavy as another cannot fly unless its wings are almost *four* times as strong. So if a bird could grow as big as a man, it would need enormous wing power and huge muscles. As it is, a bird's muscles make up more than half its weight.

In 1959 an English businessman offered a prize to any person who could build wings, take off from the ground, and, under his own power, make a figure 8 at least ten feet off the ground around

two posts half a mile apart. Many people have tried, but no one, not even a light man with light wings, has been able to get ten feet up and stay in the air more than a minute or two. And no one has managed the figure 8.

The ostrich, which is too heavy to fly, may weigh at least 300 pounds. The prehistoric pteranodon, with a wing-spread of 20 feet, probably weighed only 20 pounds.

In prehistoric times a flying reptile, called a pteranodon, had a wingspread of about 20 feet, the length of a bus. But it probably weighed less than 20 pounds. Its wingbones were hollow tubes of very thin bone, something like the cardboard tube inside a roll of paper towels.

• What's the Biggest Insect?

Two insects have wingspreads of about a foot from the tip of one wing to the tip of the other— the Indian Atlas moth and a swallowtail butterfly. A tropical insect called a walking stick is sometimes more than a foot long. Probably the biggest insect that ever lived, an extinct dragonfly, had wings two feet across.

Insects cannot be much bigger than this. Insects don't have lungs or any way of pumping oxygen to their whole body as other animals do. Air soaks into the insect's body through tiny holes. Any part of an insect's body more than a quarter-inch or so from the nearest air hole could not get enough oxygen. So even walking sticks and giant dragonflies are almost never more than half an inch thick.

• **What's the Biggest Living Thing?**

A sequoia tree named "General Sherman" in the Sequoia National Park in California is the biggest living thing on earth. It is 272 feet tall—as high as a 27-story building. If seventeen men stood in a circle and stretched out their arms, they could just about reach around its trunk. Its estimated weight is about 12 million pounds. You would need 45 of the biggest blue whales to weigh this much. If the tree were cut up into boards, there would be enough wood to make about 35 five-room houses.

The General Sherman tree has been growing for 3,000 to 4,000 years. That means it started growing back when the Egyptians were building the pyramids. The only living thing older than that, a bristlecone pine in the White Mountains of California, is more than 4,000 years old, scientists believe.

The tallest tree, taller than any other living thing, was discovered in 1964, also in California. It is a redwood, a relative of the sequoia. It soars 367 feet—as tall as a 36-story skyscraper.

Trees keep on growing as long as they live. The giant sequoias and redwoods grow so tall partly because they seem to have no enemies—except men who cut them down. Scientists do not know of any that have died of old age, sickness, or insect attack. Only lightning sometimes blasts off their tops.

The tallest tree is almost as high as the 39-story United Nations building.

• What's the Biggest Domestic Animal?

Men can change the sizes of horses and dogs, cattle and chickens by selective breeding. For many hundreds of years farmers have known how to breed animals with special qualities. Fast-running horses can be mated with each other to develop offspring for racing. To develop a breed of big horses, breeders mate big horses with other big horses. The offspring usually inherit large size.

Of all animals bred by man, the Shire horse is the biggest. A Shire horse weighs 1,800 to 2,300 pounds, as much as 12 or 14 men. The ancestors of today's Shires were the big war horses of the Middle Ages. Knights in heavy armor needed huge horses to carry them. In the 1500's Henry VIII, King of England, ordered all horses under five feet tall destroyed. Only the biggest horses were left. Descendants of these big horses have been used for a long while to pull plows and wagons and to carry heavy loads.

• What's the Biggest Human Being?

The tallest man we know about was Robert Pershing Wadlow. He was born in Alton, Illinois, in 1918. He was 8 feet 10 inches tall and weighed 491 pounds. He wore the biggest shoes ever made, size 37AA. All the clothes he wore and the furniture he used had to be made especially for him. But when he was born, he weighed only 8½ pounds, no more than many other human babies.

Human beings in the western world have been getting taller over the years. Scientists have found fossils of early men which show that some of our ancestors over a million years ago were only about 4 feet 6 inches tall. Knights of the Middle Ages must have been smaller than today's Europeans; their armor is too small for most European men today.

Recently people have been getting taller faster. In one American college 18-year-old boys today average about 5 feet 10 inches tall, an inch taller than the average boy at the same college 29 years ago. American college girls are taller too.

French, English, Danish, and Italian children are all bigger on the average than their parents were at the same age. But Americans and Japanese seem to have changed most in height. Americans' average height has gone up almost an inch in 30 years. If people had grown an inch every thirty years since the prehistoric men of a million years ago, we would be half a mile tall by now.

Scientists do not know why people suddenly are getting so much taller. One reason may be that we have better food and life is easier today. Also in the last hundred years peoples of the world have moved around more—from the country to the city, from one city to another, and from one country to another. Some scientists think that when peoples from different parts of the world marry, the children are likely to be bigger than their parents. Perhaps it is because people from all over the world meet here that Americans, on the average, keep getting taller and taller.

On the other hand, the tallest groups of people in the world hardly move around at all. Men of the Watusi and Dinka tribes in East Africa and the Ona Indians of Chile average over 5 feet 11 inches. But the children are about the same height as their parents. As a group they are not getting taller.

• ## Is There a Limit to Bigness?

If we grew too big, our bodies would be too heavy and too complicated. A giant of the fairy tales, ten times as tall as a man, could not look like us. If he were 10 times as tall as a man, say 60 feet tall, he would also be 10 times as wide and 10 times as thick. That means he would weigh 1,000 times as much as a man (10 times 10 times 10) or about 150,000 pounds. To hold up all this weight his legs would have to be much thicker so they would not be crushed and much shorter so they would not bend under his weight. To hold his giant hand, he would need arm bones so short and thick they could hardly move. His other bones would have to be thicker and shorter too. He would barely be able to drag himself around.

A giant's internal organs would have to be more complicated too, just as ours are more complicated than those of a mouse or of a bird. A giant weighing 1,000 times as much as a man would need to absorb 1,000 times as much food through his intestines and 1,000 times as much oxygen through his lungs. But the surface of his

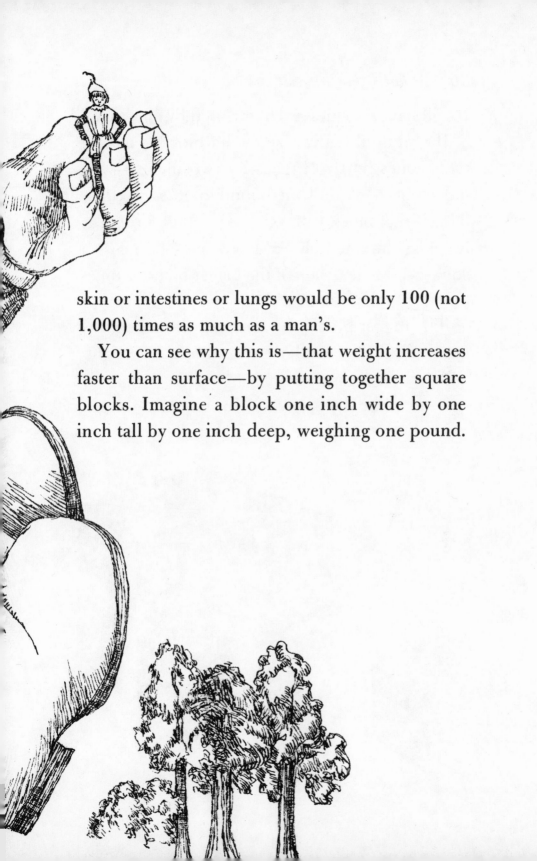

skin or intestines or lungs would be only 100 (not 1,000) times as much as a man's.

You can see why this is—that weight increases faster than surface—by putting together square blocks. Imagine a block one inch wide by one inch tall by one inch deep, weighing one pound.

It will have six sides, each one inch by one inch.

If you double the size of the block—make it two inches by two inches by two inches—you must put 8 of the one-pound blocks together. This bigger block will weigh 8 pounds, 8 times as much as the small block. There are 24 one-inch squares on the outside of the bigger block, 4 times as many as the small block has.

The bigger block, therefore, has twice the dimensions of the smaller one, 8 times the weight, and 4 times the surface.

Tiny animals can take in enough oxygen

through a smooth lung. But the intestines and other organs of bigger animals have to fold back and forth or coil around themselves to take in enough food or air for their weight. A human lung looks something like a sponge made of tiny cup-shaped hollows called air sacs. There are more than 600 million of these air sacs in a human lung. If the walls of these air sacs could be spread out flat, side by side, they would cover more floor space than the average house—an area of 2,600 square feet.

How much bigger can human beings become? Scientists are not sure. But they know we cannot keep growing bigger and bigger forever.

• Is Bigness an Advantage?

In some ways it's a help to animals to be big. A big animal doesn't get washed away in the rain or fall down small holes or get blown around by the wind. A horse can gallop over grass that an ant can barely climb over. A bigger animal has a better chance of getting away from his enemies than a small one has.

Being big also helps some animals keep warm. A warm-blooded animal always loses heat from his skin. A big animal has less skin surface compared to its weight than a small animal has. So, compared to its size, a small animal loses more heat from its body than a big animal does. A little animal, therefore, must struggle to keep warm.

To keep warm, an animal needs food. A mouse eats about one-quarter of its own weight in food

every day. We have an easier time than a mouse in keeping warm because we have less surface for our size. So we do not need as much food-fuel to warm ourselves. We weigh about 50 times what we need to eat in a day.

Big animals have another advantage; they usually live longer than little ones. The giant turtle sometimes weighs 1,500 pounds and probably has the longest life of any backboned animal. One was known to live 152 years. Some insects and other very small animals live only a day.

Big animals also have room for bigger brains. A mouse cannot learn as much as a dog because a mouse's brain is too small for that kind of learning.

Once it is big enough to work well, however, a brain does not necessarily keep getting better as it gets bigger. The whale and the elephant have brains that are bigger but not better than ours. Part of the reason is that each pound of brain must control more pounds of body. And the whale's brain, the biggest of all brains, is small for the size of the whale. The blue whale is over 1,000 times as big as a man. His brain is only about 6 times as big as ours.

So it is a help to be big. Big animals face fewer dangers. They keep warmer and live longer. Their brains can be better.

But the biggest animals are not better off than the small ones in every way. Their lungs and stomachs must be more complicated. Their hearts and blood vessels must work harder to get their blood to their heads. Their bones must be stronger.

A giraffe could not be as heavy as an elephant because his long thin legs would break under the weight. An elephant as big as a blue whale could not move his great bulk without water to hold him up.

For every kind of animal, there is a size best for it. If a mouse or an elephant or a man became very much bigger, it would stop being a mouse or an elephant or a man—and would be something quite different.

· II ·
Man-made Things

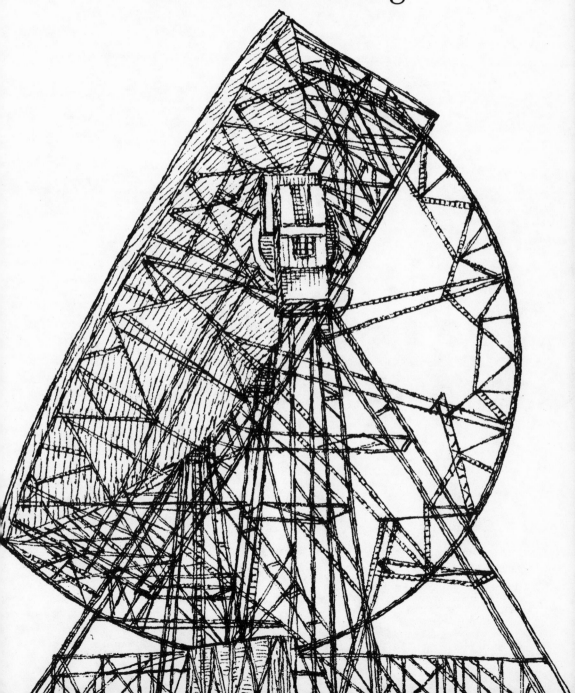

- **What's the Biggest Statue?**

A man cannot be a giant. But men have sometimes wished they could be. So to show the importance of great men and great ideas, they build giant statues.

A statue of Buddha, carved into a cliff in Bamian, Afghanistan, is tallest. It towers 173 feet high, as tall as a 17-story skyscraper and was made more than 1,300 years ago.

The biggest statue heads, the giant heads of Washington, Jefferson, Lincoln, and Theodore Roosevelt, were carved into the top of Mount Rushmore in South Dakota. Each face is 60 to 70 feet high, as tall as a 6- or 7-story building. If the bodies of the men had been carved to fit the heads, the statues would be almost three times as tall as Buddha—tall enough to look into the top windows of a 46-story skyscraper.

Mountains hold up the statues of Buddha and of the four American presidents. The Statue of Liberty in New York Harbor is the biggest statue standing by itself. It rises 151 feet from the base of the statue to the tip of the torch. (If you measure from the bottom of the stand, Liberty is 305

feet tall, taller than the statue of Buddha.) One hand is 16 feet long. If you visit the statue, you can walk up a narrow spiral stairway to the crown on Liberty's head. Workmen can also climb a ladder inside the arm to repair the nineteen lamps inside the torch.

More than 300 sheets of thin copper, weighing about 200,000 pounds, cover the outside of the statue. An iron framework holds up the copper, and steel columns support the iron frame. Gustave Eiffel, who later built the Eiffel Tower in Paris, made this framework. The whole Statue of Liberty weighs 450,000 pounds, as much as 25 big freight trucks.

• **What's the Biggest Building?**
The Empire State Building in New York City is the tallest building. It rises 102 stories high— 1250 feet—almost a quarter of a mile. (With its 222-foot television antenna, it is 1,472 feet.) Ten thousand people can work in its offices, and over 20,000 people visit it every day and use its 63 passenger elevators—almost as many people as live in a city the size of Danbury, Connecticut. The whole building weighs about 303,000 tons or 606 million pounds.

Within a few years New York may have two buildings taller than the Empire State Building. Builders are planning two 1,350-foot towers for a World Trade Center. The towers will each have 110 stories. That makes them eight stories (and 100 feet) taller than the Empire State Building. They will have 230 passenger elevators.

Can buildings keep getting taller and taller? Most engineers say a building could rise a mile high, more than four times as high as the Empire State Building. Up to now builders have not tried to put up skyscrapers as high as that.

As we have seen, if a man could grow ten times as tall, he would not look the same. He would have to have different bones, different internal organs, and a different way of breathing. As buildings, too, get bigger, the skeleton takes up more and more room. Elevator shafts help hold up the building, so the elevators have to be bigger and the columns thicker. This means that a skyscraper needs a larger proportion of the building for its steel skeleton and elevators than a shorter building would need. The Empire State Building has 7 miles of elevator shafts.

The architects of the new Trade Center skyscrapers found one way to help solve this problem. With new materials they can support some of the building's weight on the walls as well as on the steel skeleton. (They can also build more cheaply, because whole sections of the building can be made ahead of time in a factory.)

Today's architects can do new things because they have electronic computers to plan and run the new buildings. They can also use improved materials, such as aluminum and concrete reinforced with steel. Steel is ten times as strong as stone and weighs much less. The 588-foot-high Marina City apartment in Chicago, made of lightweight concrete, is the tallest building without a steel skeleton. Even when made of stone and steel and concrete, tall buildings don't weigh as much as the earth dug out of their basements.

The Pentagon building in Washington, D.C., headquarters of the Department of Defense, has the biggest office area—6½ million square feet of floor space. That's as much as about 112 football fields.

The Pentagon has five floors, a mezzanine, and a basement, and the building has five sides. (The word "pentagon" means five-sided.) To get around the outside of the building, you walk about a mile. There are 17½ miles of corridors. About 26,000 people work in the Pentagon.

The Pentagon has 45,000 telephones, the biggest private telephone system in the world. The people working in the building make or answer 280,000 telephone calls a day. If you could use only one phone for all those calls and made one call every minute, eight hours a day, it would take more than a year and a half to make one day's calls. The building's telephone cables would go around the earth six times, or more than halfway to the moon. There are 160,000 miles of them.

Even bigger than the Pentagon—almost twice as big, in fact—is the Vertical Assembly Building at Cape Kennedy, Florida. Here space engineers will put together the Saturn 5 rockets to

The telephone wires inside the Pentagon could stretch six times around the earth.

take American astronauts to the moon. It is the biggest building man has ever made.

It is less than half as high as the Empire State Building. But it has about 8 acres of floors, and it encloses more space than any other building ever put up, 125 million cubic feet—twice the volume of the Pentagon.

Four 400-foot tall rockets will be able to stand up in the Vertical Assembly Building at the same time. So that the rockets can get out, the doors of the building are 460 feet high—about 46 stories. The United Nations Building could go through one of these doors.

The biggest land vehicle ever built, called a crawler, will take the rockets to the launching pad.

• What's the Biggest Stadium?

The biggest indoor stadium is the Harris County Stadium in Houston, Texas. It is the only major league baseball field with a full roof. Its roof is a big round dome made of steel and plastic. An 18-story building could fit under it. Major league baseball players have tried to hit the roof with a ball, but, so far, they haven't been able to.

The dome, the biggest in the world, measures 642 feet across. It has 4,596 windows which let the light in while keeping the rain out. About 45,000 people can sit under the dome to watch baseball or football or rodeos.

More than twice this number—over 110,000 people—can sit outdoors in the Los Angeles Memorial Coliseum, the biggest stadium in the United States. If one person a minute went through the gate day and night, it would take more than two months to fill the stadium.

The biggest stadium in the world is the Strahov Stadium in Prague, Czechoslovakia. It can hold 240,000 people in the audience.

- **What's the Biggest Bridge?**
The world's longest automobile bridge, the Pontchartrain Causeway in New Orleans, crosses almost 24 miles of water on supports fastened in Lake Pontchartrain.

The railroad bridge across Great Salt Lake in

Utah is still longer—30 miles—and the longest bridge on earth.

The highest bridge is the Royal Gorge Bridge in Colorado, a suspension bridge 1,053 feet above the Arkansas River.

The Verrazano-Narrows Bridge, the longest and heaviest suspension bridge, crosses the entrance to New York Harbor. Suspension bridges hang on cables attached to high towers, with no

If the Statue of Liberty were next to the Verrazano Bridge, it would reach only halfway up one of the towers.

support in the middle.

The Verrazano-Narrows Bridge has the longest span, or distance between the towers, of any bridge—4,260 feet or about four-fifths of a mile. The Golden Gate Bridge in San Francisco has the second longest span, 60 feet shorter.

Engineers think a bridge may someday hold up a span almost two miles long. Bridge engineers, like building engineers, use new kinds of steel, concrete, and aluminum. Steel used today allows bridges to be lighter but twice as strong as they were 25 years ago.

The new Verrazano-Narrows Bridge has two six-lane highways hanging more than 20 stories over the water. By 1980 it will have two levels of highway, and over 30 million vehicles will use the bridge every year.

Four enormous cables hold up the 168-million-pound double deck and about 20 million pounds more of buses, trucks, and cars. Each cable is about 1½ miles long, a yard thick, and weighs more than 19 million pounds; 26,000 pencil-thin wires were twisted together to make each cable. The cables use 142,500 miles of wire in all.

These cables are attached to two towers—one on each side of the harbor entrance. The tops of the towers are 690 feet above water—more than twice as high as the Statue of Liberty. The whole bridge has enough steel to build three Empire State Buildings.

- ## What's the Biggest Tunnel?

The longest automobile tunnel cuts 7 miles under the Alps between France and Italy at Mont Blanc. The Mont Blanc Tunnel saves drivers 325 miles of winding road through the mountains. About 450,000 cars, trucks, and buses a year can drive through it—an average of almost one per minute.

The longest railroad tunnel, the Simplon Tunnel, links Switzerland and Italy through the Alps. It runs for 12½ miles. In a few years there may be a longer railroad tunnel under the channel between Japan's main island of Honshu and the southern tip of Hokkaido.

The new Chesapeake Bay Bridge-Tunnel in the United States combines two tunnels and two bridges. The tunnels and bridges together cover the longest stretch of *ocean* ever crossed by car—17½ miles of water across the mouth of Chesapeake Bay.

- **What's the Biggest Ship?**
The biggest passenger ship is the *Queen Elizabeth*.

She is 1,031 feet long, longer than three football fields, and over 118 feet wide.

The *Elizabeth* usually carries 1,200 crew members—the officers, sailors, engineers, cooks, housekeepers, and other workers who take care of the ship and the 2,300 passengers. When the big ship ferried troops during World War II, more

than 15,000 persons squeezed aboard. The *Queen Elizabeth* has enough electricity to light all the lights in all the houses in a city of 25,000 families.

The atomic-powered aircraft carrier, the U.S.S. *Enterprise,* is the biggest and most powerful ship ever built. She is 1,101 feet long, 70 feet longer than the *Queen Elizabeth.*

The *Enterprise* carries 4,600 men and 100 airplanes which land on the ship's 4½-acre flight deck. Her atomic furnaces build up 200,000 horsepower and she can sail for years without refueling.

• What's the Biggest Dam?

The Fort Peck Dam in Montana needed 126 million cubic yards of earth, stone, and steel for its 4-mile span across the Missouri River. That's enough to fill the biggest building in the world— the Vertical Assembly Building at Cape Kennedy —26 times. The main section of the Fort Peck Dam is 10,448 feet wide, as much as eight Empire State Buildings laid end to end and then some. The dam rises 250 feet high, as tall as a 25-story building. It has the biggest volume of any dam in the world. The reservoir formed by the dam covers 383 square miles.

The highest dam is Grand Dixence in Switzerland. It is as tall as a 92-story building and more than three times as tall as the Statue of Liberty with her stand.

The Kariba Dam in East Africa forms the biggest reservoir and stores the most water. When it is full, it holds more than seven times as much water as the Fort Peck Reservoir. It could supply the United States with water for four years.

• What's the Biggest Airplane?

The heaviest airplane is the Air Force's B-70. It weighs 550,000 pounds, as much as thirty big trucks. It is 185 feet long, and its wings measure 105 feet from tip to tip.

We saw above that an ostrich is too big to fly. How, then, can a big plane fly?

A big bird needs more power compared to its weight than a smaller bird needs to do the same thing. A pigeon does not have as much power for its weight as a hummingbird has, and an albatross does not have as much power for its size as a pigeon. We have seen that even with big wings a man cannot get off the ground and fly under his own power. To fly like a hummingbird, we would need an enormous amount of power.

The same scientific law applies to airplanes. A big airplane, 64 times as heavy as a little plane, needs 128 times as much power.

Airplanes today can be so big because today's engines are so powerful. New fuels and jet and rocket engines supply the power a B-70 needs to fly.

• What's the Biggest Airport?
Dulles International Airport in Washington, D.C. has the biggest area. It covers over 9,000 acres or about 14 square miles.

O'Hare International Airport in Chicago is the busiest. More than a thousand airplanes land or take off there every day. That's an average of one plane coming in or going out almost every minute.

• What's the Biggest Rocket?

In January 1964 the United States launched the biggest rocket and man-made satellite to go into space up to that time. Saturn 1 stood 16 stories high and carried 20,000 pounds of cargo. It put into orbit a load heavier than three railroad engines. Altogether, with its load, the satellite weighed 37,700 pounds, more than six railroad engines. Russian satellites carried almost as much.

But more than half the cargo, or payload, of Saturn 1 was only sand. Engineers wanted to know whether the rocket could carry this much weight. They found it could.

Engineers and space project workers are now finishing a rocket more than twice as tall as Saturn 1. This rocket is Saturn 5, which will take U.S. astronauts to the moon and back. It will be made of three separate rockets, joined together. The first stage alone will have as much power as 2,900 diesel locomotives and will hold 537,000 gallons of fuel; 250,000 nuts, bolts, and rivets (in 2,000 sizes and shapes) will hold together this first stage. The whole Saturn 5 is 365 feet high— as tall as a 36 story building—and 33 feet wide at the bottom. Engineers used the lightest materials available, but it still will weigh 6,100,000 pounds with its fuel.

• **What's the Biggest City?**
Tokyo has the biggest population; 8,302,561 people lived in Tokyo, the capital of Japan, when they were counted in 1960.

Governments usually count the population of a city or country every ten years. They call the count a census. The number of people in a city changes, of course, from year to year, so the numbers between census years are not exact. About 30,000 people come to Tokyo every month to live. By now the city has over 10 million people. Some officials predict that it may have 28 million people by 1975.

London is the second biggest city in population and New York the third biggest.

Los Angeles has the biggest area of any city. At present, Los Angeles sprawls over 455 square miles and covers more than twice as much area as Tokyo.

- ## What's the Deepest Hole Ever Dug?

The deepest mine is a gold mine in Transvaal, South Africa. This mine goes down in the earth 11,246 feet, more than two miles.

The deepest oil well was drilled in Pecos County, Texas, to 25,340 feet—almost five miles deep.

Scientists plan to drill an even deeper hole. To find out what the inside of the earth is like, American and Russian scientists hope to drill holes through the earth's crust to the layer underneath. The boundary between the two layers is called the Moho, after a man named Mohorovicic. Professor Mohorovicic discovered the boundary by studying the shock waves from earthquakes. American scientists call their hole the Mohole.

To get to the Moho through land, scientists would have to drill down twenty or thirty miles through the earth's crust. But the crust is thinner under the ocean. In some places scientists think the Moho lies only about three miles below the ocean floor.

In 1961, on a special ship in the Pacific Ocean, Mohole drillers picked up samples of the earth

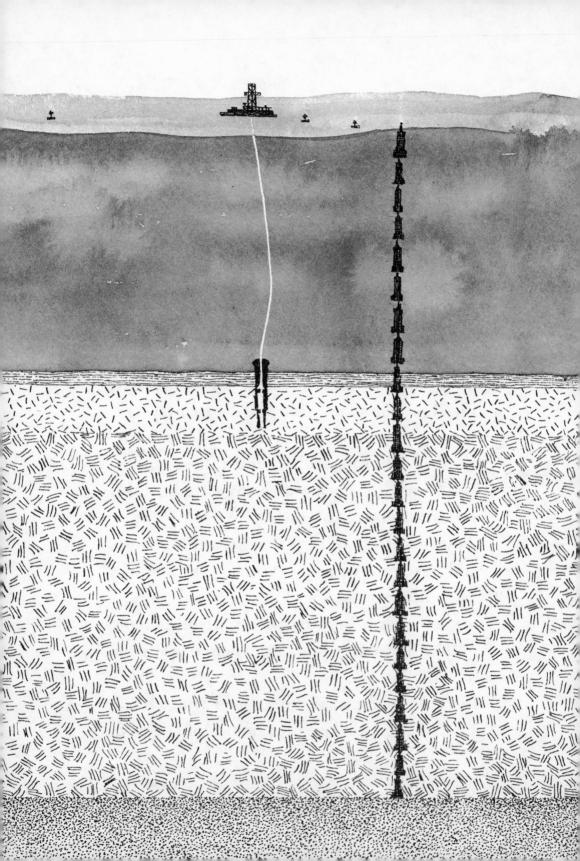

601 feet beneath the ocean floor. Some day soon scientists hope to reach the Moho more than six miles down from the surface of the ocean.

- ## What's the Biggest Computer?
  Even though architects and engineers will keep building bigger buildings, bridges, and rockets, they have stopped making bigger computers. The bulkiest computers don't do the biggest job any more. There are huge computers that take up the space of a room or even a whole building. But newer and smaller computers work faster and are "smarter."

  Designers of computers now use tiny electronic parts. Some parts are so small that 5,000 of them fit in a thimble. One computer about the size of a typewriter can add or subtract 166,000 times a second. Miniature computers, about the size of a

Between the bottom of the Mohole and the drilling rig at the surface, you could place the Empire State Building at least 24 times.

washing machine, now do the biggest computing job.

One of the most advanced computers can add 2½ million times or multiply 500,000 times in one second. This machine takes about one hour to do what a man with a pencil and paper would need almost 2 million hours to do. If the man worked eight hours a day, five days a week, it would take him 960 years to do this much work. This computer costs several million dollars or rents for more than $100,000 a month. Even at this rate it saves money for a lot of business and government projects. One dollar buys as much calculating as a man could do in a year.

Another computer can do 3 million arithmetic problems a second and can calculate 10 million times faster than a man can.

The Atomic Energy Commission has the biggest group of computers in the world in the Livermore Laboratory in California. Rooms full of computers work 24 hours a day seven days a week.

Computers have already changed almost everything we can do or make. They help find better ways to build bridges, buildings, tunnels, and dams. In the biggest buildings, computers regulate air conditioning, lighting, elevators, and almost all services. Computers help tell why traffic jams happen. They can show how rockets and airplanes will work before they are even built. They can control air traffic and handle ticket reservations for the airlines. They can find particles in the atom and help to tell what they are. Computers are perhaps the most amazing tools men have ever designed.

But there is one computer even more powerful than these. It also fits more complicated parts into a smaller space. That is the human brain.

The most complex man-made computer has about three million electronic connections. Your brain has many billions of nerve connections.

The brain's connections are hooked up like an incredibly complicated switchboard. They take about 10 thousandths of a second to go into action. A computer switch works about 10 million times faster. But the brain does something the computer cannot do. It can make a lot of different connections at the same time.

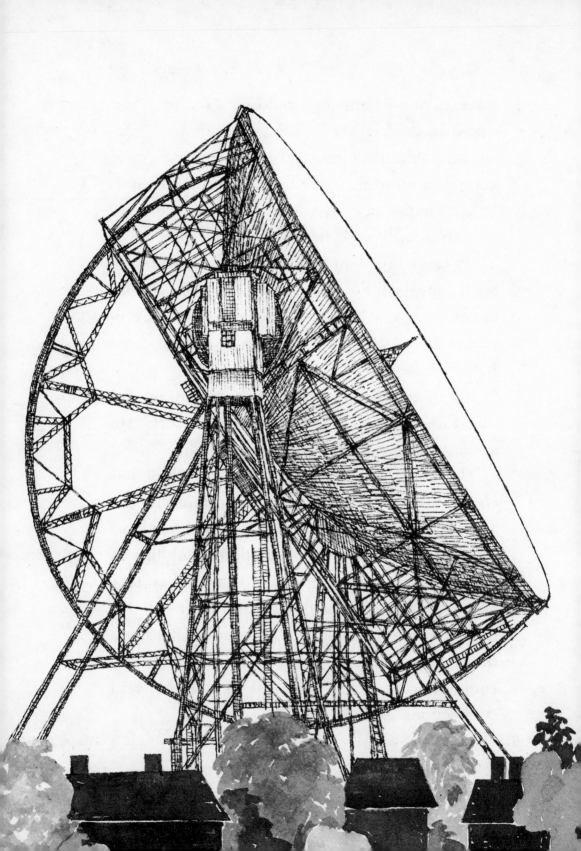

- ## What's the Biggest Telescope?

Astronomers use two kinds of telescopes to explore outer space. The optical telescope collects light waves, and the radio telescope collects radio waves. In a way, one "sees" and the other "hears."

The biggest optical telescope is the Hale Telescope of the California Institute of Technology on Palomar Mountain. The Hale Telescope, which uses mirrors instead of a glass lens, is a reflector telescope. Its "eye" is a huge mirror 200 inches across (as wide as a station wagon is long). It sees stars so far away that light takes 5 billion years to get from them to earth. One light-year—or the distance light travels in a year—is six million million (6 trillion) miles. The Hale Telescope sees stars 5 billion times as far away as that. They are 30,000,000,000,000,000,000,000 miles away.

The Hale Telescope took twenty years to build. With a special camera, it can photograph more than 30 billion stars, including some that are 4 million times as faint as any that can be seen with the unaided eye.

The radio telescope at Jodrell Bank

Radio telescopes can tune in on radio waves from outer space. Some of these radio waves come from objects in space that even the most powerful optical telescopes cannot see.

Some radio telescopes have antennas shaped like enormous saucers. The biggest fully steerable radio telescope is at Jodrell Bank, in England. Its saucer measures 250 feet across.

Even bigger is the radio telescope in Arecibo, Puerto Rico, which belongs to the U.S. Department of Defense. Its saucer-shaped antenna, 1,000 feet wide, looks like a big hole lined with chicken wire. You could lay almost two Washington Monuments end to end across the antenna, which covers more than 18 acres. It cannot be steered as the Jodrell Bank antenna can.

A radio telescope picks up radio waves from stars and other objects in space the way a television aerial picks up waves sent out by television transmitters. Radio telescopes must be much bigger than optical telescopes because radio waves are longer than light waves. Both radio waves and light waves, though, have a speed of 186,000 miles a second.

Working together, radio astronomers and optical astronomers recently found an object farther away than any ever discovered before. It seems to be something like a star which gives off radio waves. Astronomers think it is more than 5 billion light-years away.

· III ·
The Earth and the Universe

• What's the Biggest Mountain?

The highest point on earth is the peak of Mount Everest on the border between Tibet and Nepal in the Himalaya Mountains. It rises five and a half miles above sea level. This is so high that the air gets thin at the top. The earth is covered by a blanket of air that gets thinner and thinner as you go up. Climbers who wish to reach the top of Mount Everest carry oxygen to breathe in the thinner air.

Mount Everest and other mountains are usually measured from sea level. If we measure from the base of the mountain itself, the tallest mountain is Mauna Kea, an extinct volcano in Hawaii. From its base, Mauna Kea rises over 33,000 feet. That's more than half a mile taller than Mount Everest from sea level. But Mauna Kea's base is almost four miles below sea level, under water. Its top is only about 2½ miles above the sea.

Mount Everest and Mauna Kea are different kinds of mountains and became big in different ways. The Himalaya Mountains, including Mount Everest, were formed when the earth's crust wrinkled or folded. At least part of the Himalaya

Mountains must have been under the sea at one time. Scientists have found sea shells and fossils of sea animals and plants on mountain peaks.

Mauna Kea is another kind of mountain, a volcano. Where there is a weak spot in the earth's crust, hot gases and rock may push up from deep inside the earth. The rock is so hot it is liquid. When it comes to the top, it cools and becomes lava. The lava flows over the outside of the hole and hardens.

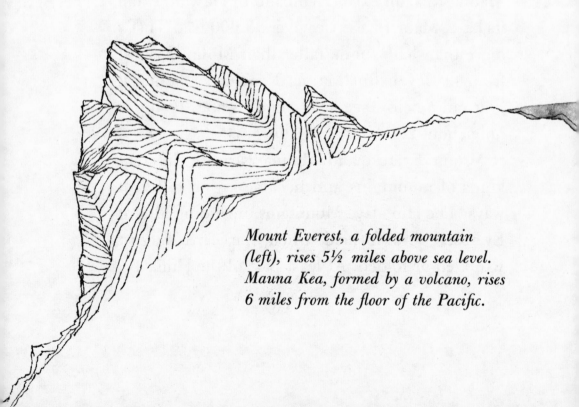

Mount Everest, a folded mountain (left), rises 5½ miles above sea level. Mauna Kea, formed by a volcano, rises 6 miles from the floor of the Pacific.

Each time a volcano erupts, the lava and ashes pile up on the layer before. So the mountain gets higher and higher. This kind of mountain can grow much faster than a folded mountain like Mount Everest. Mount Everest took millions of years to get as high as it is. A volcano can rise a thousand feet or more in nine or ten years. But most volcanoes grow much more slowly than that. It may take a million years or more to build a giant volcano like Mauna Kea.

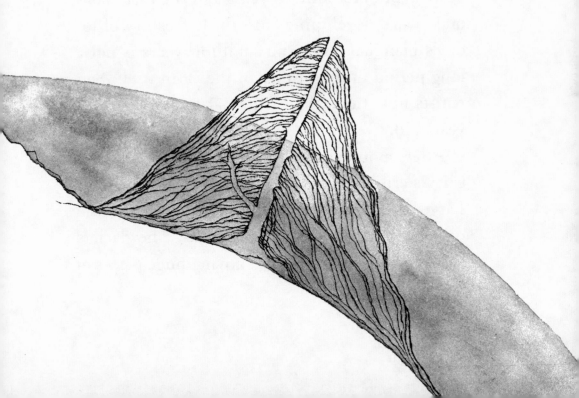

• What's the Biggest Mountain Range?

The highest mountain range on land is the Himalayas. This chain of mountains has ten out of the eleven highest mountain peaks on earth. Each of the ten, including Mount Everest, is over five miles high.

Generally the biggest mountains are the youngest. The biggest mountains of the earth—the Himalayas, the Rockies, the Alps, and the Andes, —were formed within the last 60 million years.

Sixty million years is a long time compared with man's history on earth. The most primitive man we know of lived less than two million years ago. Sixty million years ago the first mammals were developing into the ancestors of today's mammals. But sixty million years is not a long period in the history of the earth itself. Scientists now think the earth is at least 4½ billion years old.

After mountains have pushed up from the earth's crust, water begins to wear away the tops. Large blocks of ice and snow, called glaciers, form on the tops of many high mountains. The glaciers slide down the mountains, shoving huge pieces of rock and earth along with them. The Appalachian Mountains in the United States are much older than the Himalayas. The Appalachians are over 200 million years old. Since they were formed, rain, snow, and wind have worn down their peaks into low rounded hills.

The oldest mountains of all have disappeared. They have been worn down to flat land. Some mountains on the moon, where there is no rain or snow, may be as high as Mount Everest.

Although the Himalayas are the highest mountains, the Andes form the longest chain of land mountains. The Andes stretch 4,500 miles along the coast of South America. That's farther than the distance across the United States from the Atlantic to the Pacific.

In 1958 scientists discovered an even longer mountain range called the mid-ocean Ridge. It lies under water in the center of the oceans between the continents. If you had a tape measure long enough to wrap twice around the earth at the equator, you could use it to measure the 40,000 miles of the mid-ocean Ridge.

The main ridge loops around the globe like a

snake. It is longer and broader than any mountain system on land. In some places it is 3,000 miles wide—as far as from New York to San Francisco. A giant crack splits apart the underwater mountains, forming steep cliffs two miles high. Most of the mountain tops are under water. But volcanoes rise along the Ridge, and sometimes their cones poke up above the water, forming islands. The Hawaiian Islands are volcano tops on the Pacific Ridge, and in the South Pacific, peaks of the Ridge form the Galapagos and Easter Islands. Iceland and the Azores sit on top of the mid-Atlantic Ridge.

- ## What's the Biggest Island?
  The biggest island of the United States is Hawaii, one of the Hawaiian Islands. It covers over 4,000 square miles and was built by five volcanoes, including Mauna Kea.

  Greenland is the biggest island on earth. It is a

Iceland and the Azores are peaks of a great undersea mountain range.

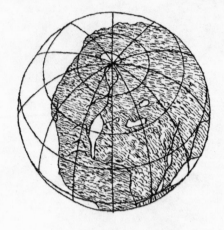

county of Denmark, although the rest of Denmark is 1,300 miles away. It covers about 840,000 square miles—fifty times as much as the rest of Denmark.

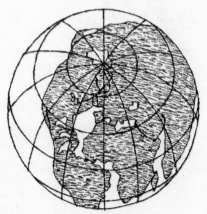

• **What's the Biggest Continent?**

The Eurasian continent —Europe plus Asia—is the biggest. It has an area of 20,750,000 square miles. It is bigger than Africa and North America together.

Do the continents change in size? Different

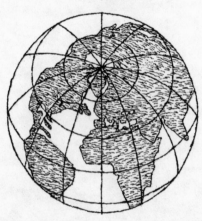

Some scientists believe that a super-continent split up into today's continents. According

scientists explain the size of continents in different ways. Some think that long ago all the continents were joined together. They believe that gradually, over millions of years, giant cracks opened across the land, which then drifted apart and became the continents as we know them.

One important scientist, J. Tuzo Wilson, has another theory. Dr. Wilson is a Canadian geophysicist, a scientist who studies the earth. He believes that continents probably start small and

to another theory, continents start as volcanic islands which grow and join together.

grow bigger. His theory is this: More than two billion years ago all the main continents started as separate islands. From volcanoes on the edges of these islands, lava came up from the center of the earth and piled up into mountains. The mountains were leveled down by wind and water and ice.

As the islands grew, they joined together and became still bigger. According to Dr. Wilson, the earth may be a little like an egg that has cracked while being boiled. The inside oozes out on the shell and hardens to form continents. This seems to have happened in Hawaii to form islands. North America, this scientist thinks, was once three separate volcanic islands. Lava cemented them together.

If Dr. Wilson is right, the continents are still growing. The islands of New Zealand—only 500 million years old—may someday join together and grow into a continent.

Either one of these two theories may be right —or wrong. Scientists still do not know very much about whether continents are getting smaller or bigger.

- ## What's the Biggest Cave?

The Berger cave in the French Alps is the deepest known cave. Explorers of this cave have gone down into the earth almost 3000 feet—more than half a mile.

The Carlsbad Cavern in New Mexico has the biggest underground room. This enormous room is 625 feet wide—twice the length of a football field. It is 4,000 feet long—thirteen football fields laid end to end. It has a ceiling 285 feet high. That's as tall as a 28-story building. Parts of the cave have still not been explored.

Mammoth Cave in Kentucky is not as deep or as wide. But it has more miles of corridors. While Carlsbad Cavern has 23 known miles of passageway, Mammoth Cave, on its five different levels, has 6 times as many.

- ## What's the Biggest Waterfall?

Angel Falls in Venezuela is the highest waterfall. From top to bottom, it is 3,212 feet, dropping without a break for about half a mile. It is more

than 1,000 feet higher than any other known waterfall.

The 130-foot Guaira waterfall, or Sete Quedas, has most water. It is on the Alto Parana River between Brazil and Paraguay. Every second 470,000 cubic feet of water rushes over it. That's more than twice as much as goes over Niagara Falls.

● **What's the Biggest River?**

The longest river is the Nile. It runs about 4,150 miles from central Africa into the Mediterranean Sea.

But the Amazon, not the Nile, has most water. The biggest river in North America, the Mississippi, could supply enough water for New York, Chicago, Los Angeles, and the next 25 biggest cities in the United States. The Amazon has more water than the Nile, the Mississippi, and the big Chinese river, the Yangtze, put together. It has almost six times as much water as the

Angel Falls is twice as high as the Empire State Building.

Mississippi. The Amazon could supply all the people and industries in the United States with what it pours into the Atlantic Ocean.

Scientists found another kind of "river" in 1958. It is a current, called the Cromwell Current, more than 300 feet down in the Pacific Ocean. It flows in the opposite direction from the currents on the surface of the water. It moves along the equator to the east and carries a thousand times as much water as the Mississippi. This undersea river is 250 miles wide and hundreds of feet deep. Scientists believe it may be 7,000 miles long.

- **What's the Biggest Lake?**

Lake Superior, one of the five Great Lakes, covers more area than any other fresh-water lake. It has 31,820 square miles, an area about the size of South Carolina. But Lake Baikal in Siberia, which is deeper, contains more water than any other lake. At its deepest spot, it goes down more than a mile. It contains almost 300 cubic miles more water than the five Great Lakes put together.

(Imagine 300 containers of water, each a mile long, a mile wide, and a mile deep.)

The Caspian Sea, a salt-water lake between Russia and Iran, covers more area than any other inland body of water. Although it is called a sea, it is a lake because it is surrounded by land and has no outlet to any ocean. It covers 163,500 square miles, about the size of California.

For several hundred years the Caspian has been getting smaller. Rivers bring it less water than it loses by evaporation. Even so, it has over 19,000 cubic miles of water, about 50 times as much as all the rivers in the United States pour into the oceans in a year.

• What's the Biggest Ocean?

The Pacific Ocean has the greatest area. It covers more than a third of the surface of the earth— about 64 million square miles. If all the continents were placed on it, there would still be room for another large continent.

The Pacific is also the deepest body of water. It averages about 2½ miles deep. But parts of

the Pacific are much deeper than that. In January 1960, the bathyscaph *Trieste* of the United States Navy, carrying two men, dived down almost seven miles. This was the deepest ocean dive man had ever made. The bathyscaph touched the ocean bottom in the Marianas Trench.

The highest point on land, the top of Mount Everest, rises more than 12 miles above the lowest point at the bottom of the Pacific. That's almost 50 times as high as the tallest building, the Empire State Building. But if the earth were the size of a baseball, the difference between the highest and lowest points would look like a faint pin scratch.

• What's the Biggest Piece of Ice?

Icebergs are big chunks of ice floating in the oceans. Some rise as high as a forty-story build-

If the base of Mount Everest were at the bottom of the Marianas Trench, Everest's peak would be more than a mile under water.

ing above water, with eight times as much ice under water. The biggest weigh several million tons—as much as a whole fleet of ships. The biggest one ever seen was spotted in the Antarctic in 1956. It was 60 miles wide and over 200 miles long—bigger than the state of Massachusetts. These huge icebergs sometimes float 2,500 miles into warmer water before they melt.

Other huge pieces of ice are on land—the glaciers. Glaciers form when more snow falls than melts on mountain tops. As the snow piles up, year by year, its weight forms ice on the bottom layer. When the glacier snow and ice get about 100 to 200 feet deep, the glacier begins to flow downward like a very slow river, wearing away the mountain side. Some glaciers grow to enormous size. The Malaspina glacier in Alaska is bigger than Rhode Island. Near its center it is more than 2,000 feet thick.

The biggest piece of ice in the Western Hemisphere covers most of Greenland. This ice, called a continental glacier or icecap, is more than twice as big as Texas. In some places it is two miles thick. Every year 10,000 to 15,000 big icebergs break off it along Greenland's shores. If the whole icecap melted, it would provide enough water to keep the Mississippi River flowing for more than 4,700 years. The Greenland ice does seem to be melting slowly. If it keeps melting at the present rate, the ice will be gone in about 30,000 years.

A thin slab of ice floats over the Arctic Ocean, continually breaking up and refreezing. It is not as thick as the Greenland icecap, but it covers more than four times the area. It would cover about two-thirds of the United States.

This slab, called an ice pack, is only about ten feet thick in the winter and less in summer. This ice is melting faster than the Greenland icecap. Scientists estimate that there is only half as much ice over the Arctic Ocean now as there was 65 years ago.

The biggest cake of ice and snow is on Antarctica, around the South Pole. One huge piece of ice covers the whole continent of Antarctica. This icecap has more than 5 million square miles. It could cover the United States, Mexico, and Central America, with ice to spare. In many places it is over a mile deep. Explorers measured down 2½ miles near Byrd Station in 1958. The ice there goes a mile below sea level. Under the great mass of ice on Antarctica, there may be

There may be vast mountains under the Antarctic ice cap.

mountains higher than Mount Everest.

If the Antarctic icecap melted, it could supply the Mississippi River for more than 50,000 years or all the rivers in the United States for about 18,000 years. But the Antarctic icecap is not melting. In fact, it seems to be getting bigger.

The two icecaps covering Antarctica and Greenland store more fresh water than all the lakes of the earth combined. The ice is so heavy that scientists believe it has bent down the earth's crust, causing the land to sink. If anything could lift the ice from Antarctica, the whole continent might rise.

Scientists believe that there are at least 4½ million cubic miles of glacier ice in the world. If the ice from all the glaciers and ice sheets were evenly distributed, it would cover the earth with a layer of ice more than 100 feet thick.

But enormous as the glaciers and icecaps seem, they are small compared with the glaciers of past ages. About a million years ago, ice covered more than one-quarter of the earth's land. At one time glaciers two miles thick covered New England and moved south as far as what is now

Louisville, Kentucky. Ice covered almost all of Illinois, Indiana, and Ohio.

The earth has had cold and warm periods. Glaciers grew and shrank four times in the last million years. About 25,000 years ago the ice began to melt back again. It is still melting. Although the Antarctic icecap is growing, there is less ice over the whole earth. The ice may keep melting for several thousand years. As the glaciers melt, the seas rise. If all the ice melts, the water in the ocean will rise and New York, London, and other seaport cities will some day be under water.

Perhaps 50,000 or 100,000 years from now the ice sheets may start to grow again.

• What's the Biggest Desert?

The Sahara is the biggest desert. It stretches across North Africa from the Atlantic Ocean on the west to the Red Sea in the east. Almost as big as the United States, this great desert covers about 3 million square miles. Part of the Sahara has a hard and rocky surface, and some good farm land lies among three mountain ranges. But almost half of the Sahara is sand.

• **What Was the Biggest Earthquake?**
To measure earthquakes, scientists record their energy on an instrument called a seismograph. When an earthquake releases a wave of energy, a cylinder on the seismograph jiggles against a needle. The stronger the wave, the greater the jiggle.

Scientists compare the size of one earthquake to another on a scale numbered from 0 to 10, called the Richter Magnitude Scale. Between 0 and 1 on the Richter scale is the smallest earthquake scientists can detect. A rating of 5 means a big earthquake. Six is 10 times as big as five. Ten would be 10 times as big as 9.

The biggest earthquakes ever recorded by modern instruments were the earthquakes in Ecuador in 1906 and the one in India in 1950. Both earthquakes measured 8.6 on the Richter Scale. The Alaska earthquake in 1964 was almost that big—it was 8.4. That makes it bigger than the San Francisco earthquake of 1906 and the biggest ever measured in North America. It released 400 times as much energy as all the nuclear bombs ever exploded.

In 1755, before modern earthquake-measuring instruments were used, one of the most famous earthquakes hit Lisbon, Portugal. It broke windows more than 600 miles away. All over a million square miles people felt the shocks. The earthquake destroyed most of the city of Lisbon and killed at least 30,000 people.

• **What's the Biggest Shooting Star?**
"Shooting stars" are not real stars. They are pieces of metal or stone from space. Most of them are very small and burn up completely when they reach the earth's atmosphere 30 to 60 miles up. They are called meteors.

Some reach the earth before they burn up completely and these are called meteorites. Most meteorites are no bigger than sand or pebbles.

But scientists estimate that altogether they add about 5 tons every day to the earth's weight. This load is spread over the earth and is too small to notice, even over millions of years.

The biggest meteorite ever found is in southwest Africa. It is about 9 feet square and 3½ feet thick. It weighs about 65 tons (130,000 pounds), as much as ten big elephants.

A huge meteorite hit Quebec province many thousands of years ago and left a hole more than two miles wide and about 1,300 feet deep. The hole, which is called Chubb Crater, was discovered in 1951. Scientists think the meteorite that gouged out the hole weighed thousands of tons. When it hit the earth, it was so hot that most of it probably turned into vapor. Its great heat must have burned the earth for miles around.

In 1956 and 1957 scientists saw from an airplane two giant holes in the earth which they think might also have been made by meteorites. Both are in Canada. One, in Saskatchewan, is more than 7 miles across. The other, a 400-mile-wide hole on the shore of Hudson Bay, may have been made by a meteorite hitting at an angle. If it really is a meteorite crater, it is bigger than the biggest known crater on the moon, which is 183 miles wide.

- **What's the Biggest Planet?**

Of the nine planets, including the earth, which circle around the sun, Jupiter is the biggest. The distance through the middle of Jupiter—its diameter—is about eleven times as much as the earth's diameter.

Jupiter's volume is 1,300 times as great as the earth's. You could put 1,300 earth-size planets into a ball the size of Jupiter.

Although Jupiter takes up 1,300 times as much space as the earth does, it contains only 317 times as much matter. Matter is what things are made of. A sponge big in size may be light in weight because there is so much space between the fibers. The matter in Jupiter is more spread out than the matter in the earth.

It would take only 317 earths to weigh as much as Jupiter. But astronomers usually don't talk about how much a planet or a star "weighs." If a star has more matter in it than another star, they say it has more "mass" or is more "massive."

You can compare two weights only at the same place on the earth, because weight depends on the earth's gravity. Your mass is the same wherever you are. But your weight gets less as you go into space away from the gravity of the earth.

In 1963 astronomers discovered a planet outside the solar system, as massive as 1½ Jupiters. Astronomers call it Barnard's Star B because it was first believed to be part of Barnard's Star. But they now think it is a planet, not a star.

A star is made of gas and is hot enough to shine by its own light. A planet is solid and rocky and too cold to glow with its own light. But if a planet gets much bigger than Barnard's Star B, the outside layer becomes so heavy that it crushes the atoms inside. Then the rocks get hot and become gases. They begin to glow—and the planet has become a star.

Jupiter (right) *is big enough to hold 1300 planets the size of the earth* (top right). *The sun* (shown in part on both pages) *is big enough to hold 770 planets the size of Jupiter.*

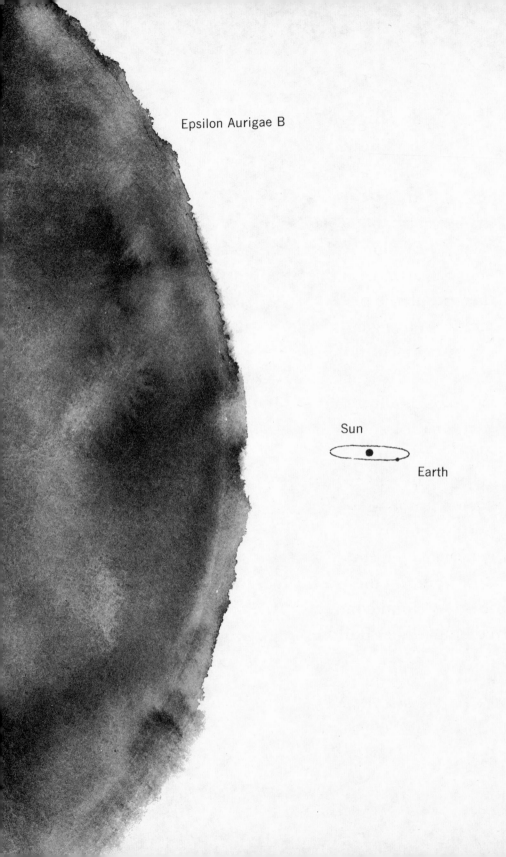
Epsilon Aurigae B

Sun

Earth

• What's the Biggest Star?

The biggest known single star is called Epsilon Aurigae B. It is almost 2 billion miles in diameter —2,000 times the sun's diameter. (The sun's diameter is about 110 times as much as the earth's.) Epsilon Aurigae B is so big that the sun and the earth, with the 93 million miles between them, could be placed almost 20 times across the middle of this giant star.

Astronomers think even the biggest stars are only about 100 times as massive as the sun. (The sun is 330,000 times as massive as the earth.) A star more massive than this, they think, either explodes or begins to shrink.

Stars, like living things, have life spans and change as they get older. Scientists think stars are born when tiny particles of dust in space swirl together in a big cloud-like ball. As more and more dust collects, the gravity becomes stronger and the dust cloud contracts, becoming smaller. The cloud particles build up pressure as they squash

Epsilon Aurigae B takes up as much space as 8 billion stars the size of the sun.

together. The pressure makes the dust cloud hotter and hotter until it begins to glow as a star.

If the pressure is too great, the star may get so hot it explodes. As the star burns up its fuel, it shrinks still more until, after billions of years, it becomes as small as a planet. It is then white hot and is called a White Dwarf. The atoms in a White Dwarf pack tightly together, making it enormously dense.

Everything is made up of atoms. Atoms are particles so tiny that there are billions and billions of them in a drop of water. But each atom is like a miniature solar system. The nucleus, or center, is like the sun. Whirling around the nucleus at fantastic speeds are the electrons, almost weightless electrical charges.

Tiny as the atom is, it is mostly space. If you could take the space out of your body and squash together the nuclei and electrons in the atoms, you would be as small as a grain of sand. But that "grain" would weigh as much as you do now.

Recently astronomers think they have found stars heavier than White Dwarfs. Even in a White Dwarf there is some space between subatomic particles. If, after exploding, a star collapsed still further, its subatomic particles might change to neutrons. The neutrons would pack together even more tightly than the atoms in a White Dwarf.

Scientists have clues that such stars do exist. They call them neutron stars. If a star like the sun collapsed into a neutron star, all the matter that is now in the sun would be squeezed into a ball about 10 miles in diameter. A cubic inch of such a star would weigh 100 million times more than a cubic inch of a White Dwarf. It would weigh 35 million tons.

• How Big Is the Universe?

It is hard to imagine numbers like a million or a billion. It is even harder to imagine distances so great that we measure them by the distance light travels in a year, going at 186,000 miles a second.

Let's imagine a football-field model of the universe. If the sun were the size of a ping-pong ball, then one inch would represent about one million miles. The earth would be a speck one hundredth of an inch across. Pluto, the farthest planet from the sun, would be the length of a football field away from the sun. Most of the solar system, we could see from this model, is space. There are only a few specks sprinkled around in it.

Our sun (with its planets) and other stars are bunched together in a group called a galaxy—the Milky Way. The star nearest to the sun is Proxima Centauri, which is about 4 light-years away. If you streaked toward that star at 17,000 miles an hour—the speed at which astronaut Gordon Cooper's capsule orbited the earth—you would need about 177,000 years to get there.

If we kept our football-field model of the solar system, Proxima Centauri would be 400 miles away. With this model, where an *inch* equals a million miles, many stars of the Milky Way would be millions of *miles* away.

Our galaxy, the Milky Way, contains about 100 billion stars. To look at them for one minute each would take you about 190,000 years.

The Milky Way is only one of billions of galaxies, each with billions of stars.

Now let's try to picture another model. The Milky Way is about 100,000 light-years across

(500 quadrillion miles). If we shrank the whole Milky Way to the size of the New York World's Fair—about 1½ miles across—one inch would now represent one light-year or about 6 trillion miles. Each star would be much smaller than a speck of dust, so small we couldn't see it except through a microscope.

Other galaxies would be like other fairgrounds, from two to thirty miles apart. The space between galaxies would be even emptier than the empty-looking fairgrounds. An American astronomer estimated that if all the matter in space was not concentrated in suns and stars and planets but spread out evenly, there would be only a few atoms in every square yard of space. In the most perfect vacuum we can make on earth, where we remove all the matter we can, including air and bacteria, there are still billions of atoms in each square yard of space. Space is so enormous that even with all the billions of stars it is almost empty.

With the fairground model, where an inch represents a light-year, the farthest galaxies astronomers have measured would be more than one-third of the way to the moon. Astronomers can now count tens of billions of galaxies. And there are probably many more galaxies beyond this. In 1964 astronomers discovered a "star," or perhaps a galaxy, over 5 billion light-years away. This is the most distant point they have yet learned about.

Scientists still do not know just how big the universe is. Does it have limits somewhere? Or is it infinite, going on and on without end? One group of scientists today thinks it has no beginning or end. But another group of modern scientists thinks that, whatever its size, the universe is getting bigger. They say that stars and galaxies are getting farther and farther apart as if they were exploding outward.

When we see something 5 billion light-years away, we are really seeing something that happened 5 billion years ago. The light took 5 billion years to get to us. This means that astronomers are really peering back into the past. Because seeing long distances is seeing back in time, scientists think the biggest telescopes may soon tell us something about the beginning of the universe— if it had one—and whether or not it is getting bigger.

Author's Note

For the statistics used in this book, I have tried to find the most accurate and up-to-date figures. But authorities often differ, and new measurements are made from time to time. If necessary, figures will be revised for future printings of this book.

Readers who would like to learn more of scientific theories about size may be interested in the following:

Men, Ants, and Elephants by Peter K. Weyl (New York: Viking, 1959)

The Wonder of Heat Energy by Hy Ruchlis (New York: Harper, 1961)

Only a Trillion by Isaac Asimov (New York: Abelard-Schuman, 1957)

View From a Height by Isaac Asimov (New York: Doubleday, 1963)

"On Being the Right Size" by J. B. S. Haldane in *A Treasury of Science* edited by Harlow Shapley (New York: Harper, 1958)

"The Size of Living Things" by Julian Huxley in his *Man in the Modern World* (New York: New American Library, Mentor, 1944)

Biomechanics of the Body by E. Lloyd Du Brul, Biological Sciences Curriculum Study, Pamphlet 5 (Boston: D. C. Heath, 1963).

BARBARA R. FOGEL

Index